1 9 4 7

A S P E N

S K I I N G

THE FIRST FIFTY YEARS

1 9 9 7

A S P E N
S K I I N G

THE FIRST FIFTY YEARS

1 9 4 7 ✳ 1 9 9 7

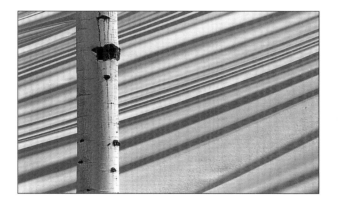

ASPEN'S LONG LOVE AFFAIR WITH SKIING

MOUNTAINS & MEMORIES, SNOW & SKIERS

RESEARCHED & WRITTEN BY PETER SHELTON

ILLUSTRATED BY ASPEN'S OWN PHOTOGRAPHERS

WESTERN EYE PRESS

WELCOME TO AN UNFINISHED STORY, *the story of Aspen skiing, which is still being written, still being lived, turn by turn, snowfall after snowfall, season after season. And this saga of skiing and skiers is woven into everything else that has happened in this once sleepy Colorado town, since it woke up after the Second World War and decided to be a successful mountain resort rather than a failed mining camp.*

For skiing is but one side, one facet, of an Aspen renaissance that's still in full swing. In no other ski resort in America has the development of slopes and lifts and ski schools gone hand in hand with the sort of visionary cultural development that has given Aspen an internationally respected music festival and music school, a physics institute, an annual design conference, the Aspen Institute for Humanistic Studies, and—big-name events and institutions aside—a vibrant town life of ideas and arts, out of all proportion to Aspen's size and relative remoteness. Ideas and arts to match its mountains. Mountains to match its skiers. And Aspen skiers who have always been the most sophisticated members of a sophisticated breed.

Of all the sports I know, skiing may be the one most concerned with beauty. The aesthetics of fresh snow, making the world new again, every morning. The anti-gravity blessings of speed and powder, flying and floating. That's one reason Aspen has succeeded so well in defining the ultimate American ski town, the ultimate American ski experience. This oasis at the upper end of the Roaring Fork Valley first attracted its modern pioneers—both ski pioneers and cultural mavens—with a natural beauty that renews itself year round. Leaves melting off the aspens in the heat of their fire-tinged fall colors. Snow sculpting a new topography that changes with every storm. Spring hauling out its gaudy painter's palettes, flowering fruit trees along every street, an explosion of flowers, meadows, electric aspen buds. Aspen is an outrageously beautiful mountain town…amid outrageously beautiful mountains. And this is where American skiing grew up.

The Aspen idea—a symbiotic fusion of sport and art, culture and nature—is still alive and well, fifty years after Walter Paepcke and his partners founded a corporation to build the first chairlifts.

Peter Shelton, who wrote this brief and engagingly unofficial history of Aspen skiing, has skied the Aspen dream since he was a young man. He knows the grand mountain shapes that mesmerized early skiers. He has skied in the tracks of the masters. He knows and loves skiing history. Aspen is a mother lode of that history.

On a foundation of old bricks and stone, of mountains close enough to reach out and touch, a maverick collection of skiing pioneers invented an experience called Aspen.

Here is that experience, condensed into a beautiful small book, condensed into 50 photographs to celebrate the 50 years that have elapsed since Aspen's first chairlifts scooped skiers off into the sky. …

Lito Tejada-Flores

THE STORY OF ASPEN SKIING, of course, begins long before the first chairlifts were installed in 1947. Rich histories always escape the boundaries of their limiting dates. Aspen skiing starts with the silver miners in the 1870s, the Swedes and Finns and Yugoslavs, who brought their "Norwegian snowshoes" from the old country to the rich strikes around Ute City, later to be called Aspen. The mining didn't stop in the winter. Deep snow slowed the mules and the ore wagons, but the prospectors still had to get around. So, they steamed and bent the tips of carefully planed 12-foot boards, attached leather straps for their boots and strode atop the snow, however deep.

Mostly, this early skiing was utilitarian. The miners skied from their diggings down to town on weekends. Kids skied to school. Mail carriers and ministers made their rounds on skis. Two early miner-skiers even tromped the 60 miles from Aspen over the continental divide to Leadville in search of oysters for a mine-camp Christmas party.

But, as all who have felt the rush of long skis gliding on snow will attest, skiing can never be purely practical. And so, Aspen's first skiers must also have raced each other down the hills, jumped the natural cornices and taken off cross country, just to see what lay beyond the next rise, skis floating them up on that sparkling, white sea.

The way it all began—
and still is, for skiers
who leave beaten path and packed slope
to adventue into Aspen's backcountry.
photo Robert Chamberlain

7

THE DEMONETIZATION OF SILVER in 1893 ended Aspen's astonishing 14-year reign as "Crystal City of the Rockies." The population plummeted. Some houses were abandoned with dinnerware still sitting on the shelves. Aspen entered its "quiet years," nearly forgotten in its high, clear valley.

Aspen languished for half a century—almost, but not quite, a ghost town—until skiing rode its white horse back into the Elk Mountains. It wasn't that simple, of course, and it didn't happen overnight. But Aspen's rebirth was in large part due to the early growth of recreational skiing in America, and to the discovery of Aspen by an extraordinary bunch of the new sport's devotees. It all started with the serendipitous coming together in 1936 of three men: Billy Fiske, Ted Ryan and T.J. Flynn.

Fiske was an adventurous New Yorker, an Olympic bobsledder schooled at Cambridge, England, and married to an English countess. Ryan, from a well-to-do Connecticut family, learned to ski in the Laurentians in the 1920s and met Fiske on a skiing trip to the Alps. At the 1936 Winter Olympics in Garmisch, the two friends wondered why comparable slopes couldn't be found in the U.S. Flynn, the third piece of the puzzle, came from mining stock, an Aspen native and a die-hard promoter of the area during Aspen's "quiet years."

Old Aspen—
period street lights,
lots of snow
and no holiday crowds.
photo Margaret Durrance

9

T.J. Flynn met Billy Fiske at a party in Pasadena, California, where he tried to sell the young man a silver mine. Fiske wasn't interested, but when he saw photos of the terrain around Ashcroft, in a canyon just south of Aspen, he agreed to come take a look. Ryan later remembered the telephone call he received from an ecstatic Billy Fiske. "'Ted,' he said, 'I think we've got it!'"

What Fiske had found, six miles from the town of Aspen at the base of 13,561 foot Hayden Peak, was snow as fine and light as any he had seen. And ski terrain that was bigger and better than anything then available at the fledgling resorts in New England or California.

In rapid order, Fiske, Ryan and Flynn formed the Highland-Bavarian Corporation, bought an old ranch at 8,500 feet at the confluence of Castle and Conundrum creeks, and built the Highland-Bavarian Lodge. They set the first beams in October, 1936, and welcomed the first guest on December 24. The lodge accommodated 16 skiers in two dorm rooms, warmed by two stone fireplaces. Three meals and transportation in Flynn's wood-paneled station wagon from the train station in Glenwood Springs were included, all for $7 per day. Ashcroft mail carrier W.C. "Bill" Tagert drove skiers from the lodge to the still-wild slopes in his four-horse sleigh at a cost of 50 cents per person each way.

Life before lifts—
earning every foot of altitude,
skiers hike a ridge of spring snow
near Independence Pass above Aspen.
photo David Hiser

EVEN BEFORE THE FIRST SKIERS arrived to test the Highland-Bavarian's promise, Fiske and company hired the popular *New Yorker* humorist, Robert Benchley, to create a brochure. Benchley, who was not much of an outdoorsman himself, called his treatise "How to Aspen." It began, "This little brochure is intended to help clear up the subject of Aspen, Colorado, both in the minds of those who know something about it already and the minds of those who have been slowly going crazy . . . hearing people talk about 'Aspen' without having the slightest idea of what 'Aspen' might be.

"Aspen," he wrote, "is a place where you can indulge in winter sports without having to get a passport, wrestle with the Atlantic, stop in Paris at the expense of your health, and come all the way back again. . . You can have just as good a time falling down there as you can on any of the European slopes. If, by any chance, you want to stand up, you can go just as fast as you could down an Alp."

Thus the legend of Aspen skiing, on the printed page at least, was born.

Aspen's early skiers spent as much time in the air as on snow, or so it often seemed. Here Friedl Pfeifer jumps for photographer Ferenc Berko.

THAT FIRST WINTER, the Highland-Bavarian partners invited Swiss mountaineer André Roch to come survey the area. Roch was at first underwhelmed by the dilapidated state of Aspen, but he soon warmed to the potential in the mountains surrounding Ashcroft. In a detailed report, Roch imagined a vast alpine complex that would include a Zermatt-style alpine village and a Swiss tram rising 4,000 vertical feet to the timberline bowls on Hayden Peak. He was convinced that Aspen Mountain, directly above the town of Aspen, could be superior to anything in the U.S. at that time, but that nearby Ashcroft, "once developed, would be a resort without any competition."

Roch also proved himself a bit of a poet, writing in his final report: "A few days later Billy Fiske, Dr. Langes and I climbed Hayden Peak . . . The slopes can be compared with the best of the Parsenn. Immense 'schusses' where your face freezes in the wind and clouds of powder snow rise behind you, make the skier seem like a rocket shooting along the ground. . . No one had ever seen more splendid skiing country before."

Hayden Peak—towering over Ashcroft,
this is the summit that inspired so many Aspen ski pioneers
with visions of treeless slopes like those in the Alps.
photo Burnham W. Arndt

PART OF ROCH'S JOB THAT WINTER was to give ski lessons, which he did both at the Highland-Bavarian Lodge and closer to town on Maroon Creek Road for the local townspeople. At the time, few Aspenites skied, but as Ted Ryan said, Roch "put the spark of skiing into the natives of Aspen."

Two who had already done quite a bit of sliding on their own were Frank and Fred Willoughby, whose father managed the Midnight Mine on the backside of Aspen Mountain. They'd been skiing the wide-open slopes above the mine in Little Annie Basin since they were kids. The Willoughbys took hungrily to Roch's instruction, and early in 1937 joined with him to form the Roaring Fork Winter Sports Club, later renamed the Aspen Ski Club.

Learning to ski—
the Durrance kids, Davy and Dicky, in galoshes,
brave the T-bar up the Little Nell practice hill.
photo Dick Durrance

But André Roch was still not done. Before he returned home to Switzerland that June, he convinced the Ski Club that with the Highland-Bavarian's grand plans still a few years from realization, they should cut a ski trail on the north side of Aspen Mountain, one that would come right into town. Frank Willoughby recalled that Roch "impressed on the club a need for a difficult but excellent downhill race course to attract publicity for Aspen skiing."

Roch scouted the route, and Frank Willoughby, who had been elected president of the club, led crews of volunteers that summer to cut the trail, which was 6,600 feet long and never more than about 50 feet wide. Aspen's lumber merchant and undertaker, Tom Sardy, remembered Willoughby coming "down from working all day at the Midnight Mine with a miner's hat on, with a light, and he was up there cutting trails by himself. He was going to get that thing done! And he did a job, believe me."

Roch Run did indeed put Aspen on the skiing map. The Ski Club hosted the Rocky Mountain Championships there in 1940 and the National Championships in 1941.

André Roch—the noted Swiss mountaineer and snow expert,
with a couple of friends, standing in front of his handiwork,
Roch Run, tumbling down the face of Aspen Mountain.
photo Margaret Durrance

But one more thing had to be done before Aspen could be called a ski town. In order to teach beginners and attract skiers who might not want to hike the full vertical of Roch Run, Aspen needed a lift. So in that halcyon summer of 1937, the Ski Club built the "boat tow," a Rube Goldbergian setup involving two wooden sleds, each with a capacity of ten riders, one sled going up while the other came down, two old mine hoists and a Studebaker motor to drive the cable. The boat tow served only the last pitch of Roch Run, and occasionally a loaded boat slid off course and tipped its startled passengers into the gully. But people loved it, happily forking over the ten cents a ride the Ski Club charged.

WORLD WAR II CAST ITS SHADOW OVER ASPEN. In 1939, Billy Fiske became the first American RAF pilot killed in action in World War II (in the Battle of Britain). Fiske's partner Ted Ryan offered the Highland-Bavarian land to the U.S. Army ski troops for one dollar for the duration of the war. The Ashcroft ski area project was put on hold…and never revived.

A few U.S. Army mountain troops did train briefly in Ashcroft during the summer of 1942, but the high valley was deemed too far from the nearest rail access. Instead, for its primary training site, the Army chose Pando, soon to be known as Camp Hale, about 70 miles northeast of Aspen across the continental divide.

Before chairlifts,
there was
the boat tow.
Friedl Pfeifer
(at left) and a full
boatload of skiers.
photo courtesy
Aspen Historical
Society

For R&R on weekends, some of the mountain troops drove around to Aspen. Laurence Elisha, proprietor of the Hotel Jerome, the only working hotel during those "quiet years," offered a room and a steak to 10th Mountain soldiers for one dollar. The boat tow kept running throughout the war, and those soldiers who still couldn't get enough skiing, hiked to the top of the mountain for the full descent, 2,700 vertical feet, on Roch Run. After skiing, Elisha served up his infamous Aspen Crud, a wicked concoction of brandy in an ice cream shake.

One of the soldiers most impressed with Aspen was the Austrian champion Friedl Pfeifer. His first glimpse came on a training march over from Camp Hale. In his 1993 autobiography, *Nice Goin': My Life On Skis,* he wrote: "We had worked our way over Red Mountain and crossed Hunter Creek. We were ordered to fall out and shave, the captain wanted us to look good when we marched into Aspen. Even as the townspeople cheered our arrival, I was filled more with the beauty of Aspen than I was proud of our accomplishment. The mountain peaks looming over the town made me feel like I was returning to St. Anton."

Pfeifer imagined Aspen growing up after the war as a "skiing community," much as his bucolic home town had come alive and thrived, thanks to ski sport, in the 1920s and '30s. He attended a meeting of Aspen's town council and told them as much, told them that if he survived the war he'd be back to help with the transformation. Aspen's town fathers weren't sure what to make of this wiry foreigner with the slicked-back hair and a visionary glint in his eye.

Ski troops of the 10th Mountain Division—
marching down Main Street in Aspen.
photo Margaret Durrance

When Friedl Pfeifer made it back to Aspen after the war in September, 1945, he found the town much as he'd left it. A population of 600 (down from a high of 15,000 at the height of the silver boom). Most of the stately Victorian buildings falling down or boarded up. A mere 40 guest rooms, most of them at the Hotel Jerome. One ski run, the narrow and very challenging Roch Run. One ski lift, the very limited boat tow. It was not a lot to work with in creating a great ski resort.

Friedl's list of needed improvements included cutting new trails, adding a beginners' rope tow, building a restaurant on the mountain, and establishing a ski school. He also wanted bottom-to-top chairlifts, like Sun Valley's, reasoning that "few people would be willing to drive 250 miles from Denver to ski a hill with a small lift." All of this, he figured, would cost upwards of $250,000. He needed investors. And he would find them, but not immediately.

Friedl Pfeifer—
early ski school
director and
dashing figure
on the mountain.
Possibly more
than anyone else,
Friedl deserves the
credit for bringing
modern skiing
to Aspen.
photo Ferenc Berko

Pfeifer was able to scratch two items from his list that first autumn. With help from Ski Club volunteers, Roch Run was widened and several new routes down the mountain, some of them a good deal friendlier to intermediate skiers, were cut. Then Friedl set about forming his ski school. Johnny Litchfield and Percy Rideout signed on, both former instructors in Pfeifer's Sun Valley ski school and fellow 10th Mountain veterans. When the first snow came on December 18, the ski school was ready for business. Unfortunately, there wasn't any. Scrambling, Pfeifer offered free lessons for housewives, and about 30 appeared the next day.

"Finally," Friedl wrote, "a Mrs. Nichol showed up. She was a marvelous 70-year-old woman, who was staying in one of the Victorian rooming houses on Third Street. She started coming out every morning for her ski lesson. Her hands usually gave out when she rode the rope tow, but nevertheless, she kept at it. We flipped coins to see who would have the privilege of teaching her and getting paid."

Lunch time—
at the base of
Aspen Mountain
in 1952,
before the era
of pasta, pesto
and Chardonnay.
photo Mary Hayes

A HANDFUL OF SKIERS, a ski school and a simple lift do not a world famous ski resort make. The missing element, it turned out, was Walter Paepcke. A decade earlier, Elizabeth Paepcke, the vivacious wife of Chicago industrialist Walter Paepcke, had invited some friends from Washington, D.C., to the couple's ranch south of Denver. When they opened the kitchen door, they found the place flooded; the pipes had frozen, then burst. And so, while Walter, who cared little for physical adventure, stayed to deal with the mess, Elizabeth, on a lark, took her friends to Aspen. She'd always wanted to see the place.

They arrived at the Hotel Jerome around midnight in a storm. Snow drifted onto the third-floor stairs from a broken skylight in the roof. The next morning they went skiing. Elizabeth tells the story in the book, *Aspen: The Quiet Years.*

"In order to go skiing , we had to get into the miners' truck with the miners. . . There were sixteen men working the Midnight Mine, including one of the Willoughbys. . . We stood up all the way up the road to the Midnight Mine. Halfway up the mountain, we got out, put seal skins on our skis, then herringboned up Little Annie Basin. . . There wasn't a track anywhere. Not a deer, not an animal, nor a man in that pristine snow. . . When we reached the top, we found a huge fir tree . . . out of the snow and the wind. We ate our lunch while looking out over the landscape. As far as we could see, the world was newly made, and it was as though the world had first begun. We felt that somehow, we were the first human beings. We could look across the range of mountains where the snow was blowing veils off the peaks. It was the most beautiful sight I've ever seen."

"We could look across the range of mountains
where the snow was blowing veils off the peaks.
It was the most beautiful sight I've ever seen." —Elizabeth Paepcke
photo Burnham W. Arndt

For years, Elizabeth ("Pussy" to her friends) tried in vain to get her husband to visit Aspen. He was busy running the Container Corporation of America and thinking up ways to integrate modern design, and modern art, into the world of commerce. CCA made cardboard packaging. And Paepcke had created a stir early in the era of mass marketing using bold, modernist graphics in his company's magazine ads.

He was also intrigued by the Greek concept of the complete life: a combination of work, play, humanistic high culture and educational leisure. Paepcke believed that mid-century industrial America was out of balance and that a conscious recombining of art and life, of intellectual and physical activity, could right the cultural ship. Following the war, and riding a wave of business successes, he had in mind to create a summer university or cultural festival somewhere far from urban distractions.

When Walter finally saw Aspen, in the spring of 1945, he knew he had found the perfect setting. And, in fact, the Paepckes' vision quickly grew to encompass a whole new community based on their cultural ideal. Their friend Marquis W. Childs summarized: "Here was to be another Renaissance, with Paepcke as Medici in chief." In Walter Paepcke's mind, this new Aspen would equal, even exceed, its former splendor as Crystal City of the Rockies.

The Jerome Hotel—
from the beginning, even during the Second World War,
the Jerome welcomed Aspen skiers.
photo Margaret Durrance

On only his second day in town, Walter presented Pussy with a surprise gift. "What is it?" she asked. "A house," he replied. In short order Walter bought half a dozen homes, hundreds of residential lots and one whole commercial block. Aspen's real-estate boom had begun.

Most of the properties could be picked up for back taxes. The eight-room Victorian he purchased for Pussy, once the home of Aspen's pharmacist, set him back $3,500. Paepcke also took leases on the Hotel Jerome and on the Wheeler Opera House and initiated plans for their restoration.

The Paepckes wanted Aspen's renaissance to be peopled by a "high type" of person, "writers and scientists and artists and business-men," and to that end invited dozens of their friends and associates to invest there, including Bauhaus designer Herbert Bayer, University of Chicago chancellor and co-creator of the Great Books movement, Robert M. Hutchins, actor Gary Cooper and Elizabeth's brother, secretary of the Navy and advisor to seven presidents, Paul H. Nitze.

The bemused people of Aspen, still clinging to the hope that silver would someday return, were generally supportive. Occasionally, though, Paepcke's enthusiasms did seem patronizing. Like the time he offered free paint to anyone who would spruce up his house, provided the homeowner let designer Herbert Bayer choose the color. Not a single taker came forward.

Art Devlin, the leading competetive ski jumper of his generation—
soaring over Gary Cooper, his wife Rocky and daughter Maria,
on Aspen Mountain's 50-meter jumping hill.
photo Dick Durrance

ART AND LITERATURE ALONE, Paepcke realized, would not be sufficient to jump-start Aspen's moribund economy. Skiing, the physical side to the Athens-in-the-Mountains equation, would provide the answer. Friedl Pfeifer had already made strides toward improving the mountain, and a partnership seemed only natural. Friedl needed capital to build a chair lift. And although Paepcke had reservations about mass recreation, he needed skiing to help support his dreams of high culture. Early in 1946, Paepcke, Pfeifer, Johnny Litchfield, Percy Rideout and a number of other investors formed the Aspen Skiing Corporation. Paul Nitze, an avid skier, was the single biggest shareholder, contributing $75,000. Coincidentally (or perhaps not), Nitze had known Billy Fiske in the 1930s, when Fiske was so excited about the skiing potential up at the Highland-Bavarian.

In a remarkably short time, Pfeifer orchestrated the installation of what was then the world's longest chairlift—actually two chairlifts, one after the other—to the top of the mountain. Together, lifts No. 1 and No. 2 traveled nearly three miles and gained over 3,000 feet of elevation. They were both single chairs with foot rests and a blanket attached for the rider's lap. The trip to the top took about 45 minutes. Lift tickets cost $3.75 a day; a season pass sold for $140.

Heading up Aspen Mountain for the first run—
original Lift 1 after an overnight dusting of powder.
photo Margaret Durrance

Also ready for the grand opening in January 1947 was a newly refurbished Hotel Jerome, a new beginners' slope called Little Nell and a dramatic mountaintop restaurant co-designed by Herbert Bayer and 10th Mountain veteran Fritz Benedict. The 360-degree view from the Sundeck, of Mount Hayden and the fourteeners—Capitol Peak, Maroon Bells, Pyramid Peak—plus the mountains of the continental divide, was the same one that had captivated Pussy Paepcke a decade before and André Roch and Billy Fiske before that.

On January 11, the official party began. A special train arrived bearing the governor of Colorado, assorted senators and congressmen, and a huge media contingent. The mayor's daughter smashed a bottle of champagne on the first lift tower. There were ski demonstrations, jumping exhibitions, ice skating, fireworks, parades and a black tie dinner hosted by the Paepckes at the newly resplendent Jerome. A little over a year after Friedl Pfeifer returned to town, only a year and a half after Walter Paepcke first set eyes on the place, Aspen was already being hailed as "The Winter Sports Center of America."

Aspen Mountain in 1947—the line of Lift 1 is visible on the right, as are Roch Run and other early trails. A T-bar serves the Little Nell practice slope to the left, below Spar Gulch.
photo Dick Durrance

TWO EVENTS, quick on the heels of the grand opening, cemented Aspen's newfound fame in the world beyond the Rocky Mountains. In fact, the November 18, 1948, issue of *The Aspen Times* announced them both on its front page: "Goethe Bicentennial To Be In Aspen In 1949" and "Aspen Awarded Most Of F.I.S. Ski Races."

Paepcke and his friend Robert Hutchins had decided to celebrate the 200th anniversary of Goethe's birth in Aspen. They would gather artists, musicians and intellectuals from around the world to honor the great poet and, in the process, give a boost to Aspen's summer economy.

By all accounts, the fortnight was a success. Pianist Artur Rubinstein, cellist Gregor Piatigorsky and soprano Dorothy Maynor all performed in the Aspen meadows under a soaring white tent, designed by architect Eero Saarinen. Albert Schweitzer and philosophers Thornton Wilder and José Ortega y Gasset all spoke to appreciative audiences.

Dr. Schweitzer's coming was a particular coup because the famous humanist and African medical missionary had not previously consented to visit the United States. Nor would he ever come again. Pussy Paepcke reported that "since he couldn't find it on his atlas, he decided [Aspen] must be a suburb of Chicago." The long train ride into the mountains wearied him, and the altitude (7,900 feet in town) inspired this comment to reporters: "Aspen ist mir zu nah den Himmel gebaut," or "Aspen is built too close to Heaven for me."

Downtown Aspen in the '50s—
skiers walking up Mill Street to Lift 1. The large building
is the Wheeler Opera House, one hub of the cultural renaissance
that accompanied the development of skiing.
photo Margaret Durrance

As great a triumph as the Goethe Festival was, its offshoots became even more important for Aspen over time. Following the Bicentennial, Paepcke created the Aspen Institute for Humanistic Studies, which still serves as a locus for what Paepcke called the "cross-fertilization of ideas." The Aspen Music Festival and Music School opened in 1951. That same year the International Design Conference was born. Aspen's de Medici had succeeded in bringing the world to a remote Colorado backwater.

MEANWHILE, OVER ON THE SKI MOUNTAIN, preparations for the World Championships had shifted into high gear. Credit for landing the biennial races, which had never before been held outside Europe, went largely to Dick Durrance. Durrance was the finest ski racer America had yet produced, a four-time national champion at Dartmouth, 1936 Olympian and the only Yankee ever to beat the Europeans on their own turf.

Durrance came to Aspen in 1947 to work as the Skiing Corporation's first full-time general manager. Dick knew, as André Roch and Friedl Pfeifer knew, that big-time ski racing could really put a place on the map. So, he got together with Pfeifer and his assistant at the ski school, Fred Iselin, and Frank Willoughby and Steve Bradley (a Dartmouth friend who was then managing the ski area at Winter Park), "and we put together a brochure and sold the Europeans on the idea that we had a big enough mountain. We had good stuff, and we guaranteed them that we would cut trails and make it suitable for the World Championships. They bought it."

U.S. Men's Olympic Team—
in Aspen training for the 1948 Winter Olympics,
from left: Toni Matt, Leon Goodman, Dean Perkins, Gale Spence, Jack Reddish, Dave Lawrence, coach
Barney McLean, Pete Seibert, Dick Movitz, Steve Knowlton and Jim Griffiths.
photo Margaret Durrance

Competitors from 14 alpine nations flooded into Aspen in February 1950. There were still so few hotel rooms that most had to be housed with local families. Aspen's resident architect Fritz Benedict and his wife Fabi had 30 guests in their house and barn. So, the two of them slept, without heat, in the chicken brooder house.

DICK DURRANCE REMEMBERS, "I'd promised that we'd have a down-hill course that would make their eyes pop, and we did that, too. It started above Midway, which is where they start all the races now, and went down . . . into Spar Gulch (where) racers had to go side to side through a very narrow gully. I made the course so that the racers would be forced to go over jumps on the mine dumps, and then down at the bottom of Spar, I cut a small Cat road just for the race itself, barely wide enough to snowplow on, to what was called Niagara. There it broke off sharply to a thirty-five degree slope, about two hundred feet long. That was a real shaker. You almost had to come to a stop there. It was a decision-maker. It was hard to decide how much speed you could carry and still avoid flying off the whole mountain. Then from the bottom of that you crossed four roads—tremendous bumps—and then went around a mine-shaft building and to the finish. By the time you were done you'd been bounced around quite a bit."

Zeno Colo, an Italian woodcutter with legs like oak trees, won it.

Zeno Colo—
the Italian ace
who dominated
Aspen's FIS World
Championships in
1950, with his three
medals: two golds for
downhill and giant
slalom, and a silver
for the slalom.
photo
Margaret Durrance

ONE OF THE FIRST COMPETITORS to arrive in Aspen for the World Championships was a young Stein Eriksen, not yet famous but already a heartthrob and a hot slalom talent from Norway. At the first sign of snow, Stein quit his job at a Connecticut ski shop and hopped on a cross-country bus. He spent a night at the YMCA in Denver, and then came on to Aspen where he took a room at the place everyone called "The Gray House," for a dollar a night.

Stein splintered his best pair of skis the day before the slalom. They were Eriksen Streamlines, laminated hickory with bronze edges, made by Stein's father, Marius. On a borrowed pair, Stein still managed a third place finish. He hit his zenith at the 1954 World Championships in Åre, Sweden, where he won three gold medals. And then he brought his elegant style—reverse shoulders matching the line of the skis, hips angulated to the inside, feet glued together—and his trademark reindeer sweaters back to America as Aspen Highlands' first ski school director in 1958.

The FIS World Championships in 1950—
a young Stein Eriksen in the first run of the slalom.
photo Dick Durrance

ASPEN HAS HAD A STABLE FULL OF STYLISTS over the years. Dick Durrance, who was a racer first—all wind-piercing crouch and fall-line efficiency—developed a deep-snow technique he called the Dipsy Doodle. Keep in mind that powder was something most skiers avoided in those days. Skis were heavy, stiff and recalcitrant. Boots were leather and ankle high. Bindings consisted of a metal toe iron, a cable around the heel and long, leather straps wrapped about the foot to cinch the whole works down. Steering was tough enough on the packed runs.

But Durrance had figured out a way to dance relatively quick turns in the deepest snow. Long time Snowmass ski instructor Weems Westfeldt described watching Dick do his thing: "He stood in a snowplow and started pumping—first one leg, then the other, like pistons in perfect opposition. Each time he pedaled on one ski, it would dart across the hill. Before that ski got too far, he would pedal on the other one and it would dart back in the other direction. He moved like a Ping-Pong ball between his skis, all the way to the bottom. . . It was amazing. He shredded it."

The perpetually tanned Friedl Pfeifer, always very natty in a dress shirt and even an ascot under his ski sweater, combined Durrance's efficiency with some of Stein's style. With his hips well forward over his skis, ankles and knees flexed to the max, Friedl skied like a swooping bird. He made it look easy. At 30 mph, he looked like a man casually wandering his own garden party, a tray of drinks balanced effortlessly in his hands.

Showing off—
Fred Iselin and
Friedl Pfeifer
jumping in tandem
at Tourtelotte Park
on Aspen Mountain.
photo Ferenc Berko

SWISS SKIER FRED ISELIN, Friedl's assistant and partner in the ski school, played the jester to Pfeifer's stern, Austrian head man. He had the face of a handsome clown with a big cleft chin and an aquiline nose. And the face seemed always to be filled with mirth. Iselin believed that skiing, like life, should be free and easy. "Ski groovier and carvier," his ads in *The Aspen Times* used to say, "not kinky and crooked with an ache in the back." In the photo accompanying the ad, Iselin carves a turn on one ski, the other one up in the air behind him in a classic "royal christie" pose. And is Iselin pushing the limits of his skill? Certainly not. His face is buried in the pages of his own best-selling book, *Invitation to Skiing*.

Long-time Aspenite Bob Chamberlain says Iselin "never drew a serious breath in his life." He remembers a story about Fred at the Harriman Cup races in Sun Valley. "The French Canadian Pierre Jalbert went off course and into the woods where he broke a ski and knocked himself silly. When he came to, the first thing he saw was Fred Iselin by his side munching a sandwich." And here Chamberlain imitates Iselin's deep, heavily accented voice: "'Go for the combined,' he said. Which, in fact, Jalbert did, getting up and finishing the downhill on his broken ski and then, the next day, winning the slalom."

When stretch pants came into vogue in the early 1950s, Iselin liked to tell his clients, "Once, my face was smooth and my pants were baggy. Now, my pants are smooth and my face is baggy."

Fred Iselin—
the clown prince
of the Aspen
ski school, at work…
or was it play?
photo Ferenc Berko

49

ASPEN'S FIRST SKI BUM may have been 10th Mountain Division veteran Steve Knowlton. He swept floors and stoked furnaces for room and board. He worked at Mike Magnifico's ski shop, repairing and waxing well into the night. For a while he served as Aspen's garbage collector. All of which left him plenty of time during the day to ski and train with Friedl Pfeifer and the Aspen Ski Club. He trained well enough to place fourth in the inaugural Roch Cup in 1946 and later that winter to win the National Club Championship downhill in New Hampshire.

The ski bum label had to be scrapped, however, in 1949 when Knowlton opened the Golden Horn restaurant. He was a serious businessman now. Well, maybe not so serious. After dinner, Knowlton and friends staged elaborate, silly skits, often in drag. The evening's entertainment ended with a bravura falsetto rendition of the hit song "Sha-boom!"

The ski bum—
slacker or artist?
1960s ski vagabond,
Steve Miller, tests the
air near the top of Bell
Mountain, in an
image used for early
Skiing Company ads.
photo David Hiser

ASPEN MOUNTAIN, or Ajax as locals called it, had one flaw. Friedl Pfeifer knew that Aspen Mountain would never be a good hill for beginning skiers. The gentlest terrain was on top of the mountain, and even that gave genuine first-timers more gravity than they and their ski instructors would have liked. And from there, how to get them down to the bottom? The easier of the two routes down, via Spar Gulch, had served as the downhill course for the FIS World Championships. The other way, via Ruthie's Run and the Roch trail, was considerably steeper. That route would become the downhill course of the future, when the World Cup came to town in the late 1960s.

Friedl figured the thing to do was to expand to a gentle breadloaf of a mountain two miles out of town, a mountain with sustained easy pitches from top to bottom. It had no name on the map, so Friedl went to see old Martin Mishmash, a retired miner who spent his days on the bench outside the Post Office. Mishmash told Friedl that loggers used to work that mountain cutting ties for the railroad. One particular "tiehack" on the crew brought a pail of buttermilk every day to wash down his lunch. Eventually the hill became known as Buttermilk Mountain.

Others tell a variation on the story. The road leading up to the logging operation, they say, was itself paved with railroad ties. Supply wagons bumping along that road were so rattled on the uneven boards that by the time they reached the sawmill milk had turned to butter.

Buttermilk, a new mountain for Aspen—
then, as now, a learning skier's paradise, a ski pro's ideal teaching hill.
The Roaring Fork Valley looks strangely empty in this 1965 image.
photo Mary Hayes

Pfeifer bought a ranch at the base of the hill in 1953, and in 1958 he opened Buttermilk Mountain with one T-bar. Ski school still met in Rubey Park at the base of Aspen Mountain, but now Friedl bussed the beginners over to Buttermilk which soon established its reputation as Aspen's learning mountain.

ABOUT THE SAME TIME that Pfeifer was developing Buttermilk, a Harvard grad and stockbroker named Whipple Van Ness Jones was approached about building a ski area in his back yard on Maroon Creek between Buttermilk and Aspen Mountain. Jones had no intention of running a ski area when he bought his horse ranch at the base of Highland Peak in the middle 1950s. But by this time, there was a demonstrable need for more ski terrain. Aspen Mountain, a victim of its own swift success, was approaching 100,000 skier visits; lift lines sometimes stretched for 60 minutes. The Forest Service was encouraging, and site walks with Pfeifer, Dick Durrance and Fred Iselin convinced Jones that he had a real mountain to work with.

Aspen Highlands opened for the winter of 1958-59 with two chairlifts, a T-bar and a rope tow. Stein Eriksen, who had helped lay out some of the trails, signed on to run the ski school.

Highlands did almost 30,000 skier visits that first year. Whip Jones gave much of the credit to Stein, who had become, by that time, the first great skiing superstar. Everybody knew Stein. He didn't need a last name. In ski movies and television commercials and in the magazines, Stein's nordic good looks, his grace and obvious joy became synonymous with skiing.

Buttermilk meets Highlands—
at least in the photographer's long lens. This unusual view of Aspen's two, just-out-of-town ski mountains shows
the long ridge of Aspen Highlands, and the white gleam of Highland Bowl, rising high over the eastern,
or Tiehack, flank of Buttermilk. What the camera hides, is the canyon of Maroon Creek between them.
photo Burnham W. Arndt

America flipped for Stein. And every Sunday at 1 p.m., Stein performed his patented flip at Highlands. Long-time Aspen observer Martie Sterling described the scene: "He would give a wave to the crowd, roar down the course, hit the jump, stretch into a swan, turn over in midair, and land to thunderous applause." In the 1960s, Stein and others invented a vocabulary of flips and spins and royal christies which was to become the language of freestyle skiing.

Over the years, Highlands developed a maverick reputation akin to the freestylers themselves. Partly, it was the independent owner-ship; Highlands competed with the Skiing Corporation's mountains for over three decades. Lift tickets and season passes were always cheaper than at the other hills, endearing the place to locals and fostering a kind of irascible skiing counterculture, the *other Aspen*.

Partly, it was the topography: a long, sharp nose of a ski moun-tain with steep drops off either side, that appealed primarily to better skiers, especially mogul skiers. And partly, it was the quirky spirit of the place. A ski area that would nurture the ill-fated short-ski "revolu-tion" of ski instructor Cliff Taylor. A ski area that featured, as its trademark, practically, the daily ritual of ski patrollers, some of them trailing rescue sleds, jumping over the Cloud Nine restaurant deck, wide-eyed patrons and all.

Vintage Highlands—
the weekly "hot dog" contests on Scarlett's run, just above the midway Merry-Go-Round restaurant,
were legendary for their high energy and loud rock and roll. Youth-culture skiing, '60's style.
photo John Russell

IN JANUARY OF 1951, with no FIS World Championships to look forward to, some of Aspen's business leaders put their heads together and came up with the idea for Wintersköl, "a toast to winter." It was the slow time following Christmas. Jack de Pagter was tending bar at the Hotel Jerome, and Delphine Carpenter, who ran the only book store in town, decided to throw a week-long party, a "Mardi Gras in Winter Dress."

"We were bored with January, bored with being broke, and bored with nobody in town," said de Pagter. Nobody was allowed to be bored during Wintersköl's non-stop parade of costume races, fancy balls, tea dances, ski movies, variety shows, sleigh rides, Elks' bingo and, well, parades. "All residents and visitors will evidence the carnival spirit by wearing startling headgear," commanded the brochure for the 1953 event. Pictured inside was the ever-spirited Fred Iselin skiing in a jockey's cap.

The same brochure featured a picture of the 1952 Wintersköl Ski Queen, Gwen Van Derbur, of Boulder. She wore a snowflake crown and carried a ski pole for a scepter. And she could ski. In addition to looking good, you had to ski to be voted the Ski Queen.

Wintersköl—
Aspen's
midwinter bash,
a carnival in the
snow, and
always, fireworks
over the
mountain....
photo Judy Hill

BEFORE JACK NICHOLSON, before Hunter S. Thompson, before John Denver or Claudine Longet or Jill St. John, Aspen's most celebrated local was Harold Ross, the founder and editor of *The New Yorker* magazine. But Ross was an odd sort of celebrity; he resisted every effort to involve him in the seminars and discussions the Paepckes brought to his hometown.

Born in Aspen in 1892 in a little house on Bleeker Street, Ross left with his family at age 9, edited *The Stars and Stripes* newspaper for U.S. servicemen abroad during WW I, and founded *The New Yorker* in 1925. Famously disheveled, with large features and dark hair that wanted to stand straight up on his head, Ross was once described by his friend Alexander Woolcott as resembling "a dishonest Abe Lincoln." Rumpled, yes, but Ross was also famous as a perfectionist hair-splitting editor and an irreverent wit whose magazine set the standard for literary sophistication.

Paepcke was dying to have Ross participate in his cultural reform movement, and the editor did make an appearance at the grand opening of the ski lifts in 1947. But from then on, Ross made it clear when he was in town that he was "here strictly for fishing." And he spurned the Institute's every effort to reel him in.

In an *Aspen Times* story on Ross's several return visits to the mountains before his death in late 1951, Bruce Berger wrote, "he wallowed in baggy clothes, fished as much as possible, hung out with old-timers he remembered from childhood, and gave visiting thinkers the slip."

*"Self portrait
with skis"—
the zenlike quiet
of a powder day
in the making.
photo
Robert Chamberlain*

SNOWMASS SPRUNG full-blown onto the Aspen ski scene in December, 1967, a $10 million Venus. Where once only ranches stretched along Brush Creek 12 miles west of Aspen, there now was a completely planned, self-contained, destination resort: five chairlifts on Aspen's fourth and biggest mountain; one on-mountain restaurant; five lodges; 120 condos, most of them ski-in-ski-out, an innovation pushed by design consultant Fritz Benedict; a dozen private homes (all utilities underground); a conference center with a movie theater; one ice rink; four outdoor swimming pools; 21 shops and boutiques; six restaurants; and one hot-water-heated access road called Snowmelt Road.

Snowmass didn't come with the colorful history that Aspen Mountain had, but what it lacked in seasoning, it more than made up in size. At 2,500 plus acres, Snowmass is over four times the size of either Aspen Mountain or Aspen Highlands.

Snowmass, Aspen's fourth ski mountain—
one corner of a giant ski area: the last slopes of the Big Burn slanting down from the left,
the runs of Sam's Knob on the right, the Snowmass Wilderness behind, somewhere below,
Snowmass Village, and somewhere above, an ice-blue winter sky.
photo Burnham W. Arndt

Snowmass skiers discovered a new world up on the Big Burn, a mile-wide, gently tilted ballroom populated with the eerily sculpted figures of a burned-out forest. And there were the long, spacious cruising runs—Campground, Green Cabin, Naked Lady—up to four miles long and loping delightfully over 3,600 vertical feet. The place was intermediates' heaven, halfway between the sheer gravity of Ajax and the security blanket of Buttermilk.

In the 1980s, Snowmass grew again, adding previously untapped expert terrain.

New mountain manager Jon Reveal took a look at the avalanche-prone Hanging Valley and Cirque areas and challenged Snowmass' resident snow genius, ski patroller Hal Hartman, to "study this thing and figure out how to open it." Hartman told his boss it would take $10,000 in explosives and two years of snow study. Reveal said, "Do it." And suddenly Snowmass had precipitous powder glades and timberline bowls, too.

The wild side of Snowmass—
originaly known for its
wide-open cruising,
Snowmass today offers
ungroomed steeps and the
best out-of-bounds-yet-in-
bounds experience in Aspen
on its Hanging Valley Wall.
photo Tony Demin

THE SIXTIES MARKED A QUANTUM CHANGE in U.S. ski racing fortunes. Individual racers, like Dick Durrance and Buddy Werner, had done well, but by and large American skiers were looked down on, not to say dismissed by the Alpine powers: the Austrians, French and Swiss. That all changed thanks, primarily, to sometime Aspenite Bob Beattie.

In 1961, still in his twenties, Beattie brought his combative style from the University of Colorado (where he had coached the ski team to national championships in 1958 and '59) to the U.S. Ski Team, which included Aspen natives Max and Bill Marolt and up-and-comers Jean Saubert, Billy Kidd and Jimmie Heuga.

Beattie insisted on year-round training, like the Europeans, and drove his racers hard, like the football coach he had once been. He liked to shout, "When you think you're going too fast, accelerate!"

Beattie also pushed to increase American influence within the cloistered world of skiing's governing body, the FIS. He lobbied for better seeding and start numbers for American racers, and for more U.S. course setters and technical delegates. In decorous, if stifling, old-world halls Beattie's gravelly voice was frequently heard yelling, in English, for the rights of his racers.

It worked. Beattie's charges, Kidd and Heuga, took silver and bronze at the 1964 Winter Olympics, the first-ever Olympic medals for American men. Jean Saubert, meanwhile, racked up second (GS) and third place (downhill) finishes in Innsbruck.

The coach and the racers—
Bob Beattie and two members of the U.S. women's squad,
Penny McCoy and Erica Skinger,
inspect an Aspen downhill course.
photo Bob Krueger

In 1966 Beattie teamed with the powerful French journalist Serge Lang to create the World Cup of skiing, the year-long, international circuit known as "The White Circus." And in 1968, he brought the White Circus to Aspen, returning the Roch Run to international eminence.

BEGINNING IN 1981, Aspen played host to an annual World Cup downhill, "America's Downhill," the only regular North American stop on the men's tour. Four times the race was won by Peter Müller, the Swiss "Trout Fisherman in America," so called because he liked to hustle down to the Roaring Fork River after the races for a little fly fishing.

Long-limbed, supple and fearless, Müller was perfect for Aspen's course, which rewards good gliding skills up top on Ruthie's Run (where racers regularly hit 75-80 mph) and then demands tenacious turning technique on the steep face of Aztec leading to the aptly named, 160-degree Airplane Turn and on down the tricky rolls of Strawpile and 5th Avenue to the finish. "Your skis must swim down the mountain, and then you are very fast," said Peter.

In '85, during Müller's race for a third Aspen title, he briefly lost control on the steepest part of the course, cleaving to his line with one ski as the other sailed above his head, outrigger-like. The big crowd gasped as one, but Müller pulled it back down and roared on to win. In the buzz of the press corral afterward he described his run. "I push me down," he panted, "and I say 'Go, Peter, Go!' I get the race on the last four turns. I make a fantastic line. Tonight I go disco dancing."

*Racers ready—
competitors warming up
for the Roch Cup Downhill
at the top of Ruthie's Run
in 1968.
photo Robert Chamberlain*

WALTER PAEPCKE DIED in 1960. And with his passing ended the most ambitious and idealistic phase of Aspen's rebirth. Aspen still blended, to a degree no other ski town in America has approached, arts and athletics, intellectual self-examination and the pure exhilaration of the mountains. But, the times they were a changin', and Aspen the recreational magnet overshadowed Aspen the cultural beacon.

Demographics changed. Leisure classes on both ends of the economic spectrum arrived to stake their claims. Extravagant homes with even more extravagant views began to dominate the skyline on Red Mountain north of town. And at the other extreme, ski bums streamed into town "lemming-like," according to *The Denver Post* circa 1965, "for a little work and a lot of skiing and kicks."

According to some, this was a different breed of ski bum, not like the hardy post-war souls who turned abandoned cabins into dorm space. Those first fanatics spread hay on the floor to temper the cold and barricade the doors against the town's roving bands of Saint Bernards. "Skiing was what we were there for," wrote Dolores LaChapelle, a school teacher and ski instructor in the 1950s. "All else came second in those first years—work, the daily hassles of getting along, sex, and material possessions except for skis." Ah, the good old days.

Looking at race results—
Roch Cup Salom, 1964.
photo Robert Chamberlain

In a more prosperous Aspen, the new ski bums of the Sixties—
with their long hair, rock music and Cold War fatalism—were viewed
as threatening. LIFE magazine even sent a writer/photographer team
to report on *"Aspen's Awful Surfer Problem: Vagabonds from the
beaches congregate at a famed ski resort."* "Drinking and pretty girls,"
ran one caption, "rank ahead of good snow to the surfers-turned-
skiers in Aspen."

But Aspen was just reflecting the changes in America at large.
Some of the "surfers" moved on, and some stayed. The LIFE crew
apparently didn't talk with ski bums Buzzy Bent or Joey Cabell,
champion surfers from Hawaii, who would start the Chart House
restaurant chain, with just four tables, over by the Little Nell in 1961.

NOT EVERYONE considered the youth culture a problem. "Aspen
Eddie" Gregorich, born to a mining family in 1917, is quoted in
Aspen: The Quiet Years: "…the town was full of hippies, long hairs,
crazies. It was lots of fun. Oh, I loved it, I'll tell ya. I like them
people…I like Aspen today. I like these young kids. Who the hell
wants to look back? Never mind what you did twenty years ago—look
for tomorrow."

Transplanted surfer—
Tommy Lee, one of the big-
wave riders from Hawaii
who frequented Aspen
in the '60s, skis by Braille
in Maroon Bowl,
off Highand Peak.
photo Robert Chamberlain

ONE OF THE WILDEST KIDS in the 1970s was Aspen's own Andy Mill. A Little-League star and then an all-state quarterback at Aspen High School, Mill was also a skiing prodigy, making the U.S. Team development squad at age 16. Precocious and rebellious, he resisted authority, took chances, got himself hurt.

He was a speed merchant, a downhiller with shaggy hair flying out from under his helmet. He raced at the edge and, all too often, over it. On Aspen's World Cup downhill course once, he caught big air off one of the roads, doing maybe "60 or maybe 65 miles an hour… Went 100 feet in the air. And landed on my back."

Over his career, including seven years with the A Team, Mill had eight knee operations, two broken legs, two broken arms, a broken tailbone and broken vertebrae in his neck and back. And still he was the top U.S. downhiller from 1974 to 1981. His most glorious finish came at the Olympics in Innsbruck, Austria, in 1976. On a training run, Mill fell hard and severely bruised his leg at the boot top. On race day, he inserted pieces of cardboard between his lower leg and boot to better distribute pressure over the injury. Then he froze his leg, "just sat down and packed snow all around it until it went numb." In the clamorous aftermath of hometown hero Franz Klammer's victory, Mill's courageous sixth place finish—the best ever to that point for an American man in downhill—was all but lost. "But it was like a victory after all I'd been through," he said.

Steep thrills—
Aspen has hosted every
kind of ski race, but it's
always been a
downhiller's mountain.
Since 1981 "America's
Downhill" has been a
regular stop on the men's
World Cup tour.
photo Alan Becker

Andy Mill came home in 1981 and built a new life out of the pieces of his ski career. He starred in his own syndicated ski instruction series. He got himself gigs doing color commentary for the networks. And he married the greatest American-born woman tennis player of all time, Chris Evert. Now Andy chases vainly but gamely after Chris' forehand smashes, and Chris works diligently to lay her improving parallel turns on top of Andy's rambunctious, effortless track. They have a house in Starwood with a view of all four mountains—left to right: Aspen Mountain, Aspen Highlands, Buttermilk, Snowmass—out the front windows. "I still can't believe we live here," says Mill. "Do I live in a fairy tale?"

ANOTHER ASPENITE to soar in the world of ski business is Klaus Obermeyer. Klaus started early with Friedl Pfeifer's ski school and became one of its top instructors. But ski instructors never made much money, especially then, so Klaus was always looking for something extra to do. "It was so poverty-stricken around here," he used to say, "everybody did something else on the side."

Legend has it that Klaus was hawking string ties to his clients in the ski school line-up. Gary Cooper, a regular on the mountain then, said to Obermeyer, "So, I see you are a businessman." And the rest, as they say, is history.

Tripping the white fantastic— Klaus Obermeyer testing ideas in his Aspen Mountain laboratory.
photo Ferenc Berko

Klaus' first skiwear triumph (after the string ties) was the quilted down parka. He came up with the idea, he says, "because I kept losing my students. They kept getting so cold going up that damn lift." So, Obermeyer cut up down comforters and sewed them into jackets. The first ones "looked like the Michelin Man," he admitted. "It was a pretty primitive thing, but, by God, it worked." The lines got slimmer, and to date, he's sold over a half million of them.

More firsts. Klaus' company, Sport Obermeyer, came out with the first ski gloves shaped like a hand. He invented mirrored sunglasses. He distributed the first real sun screen, which was developed by Friedl Pfeifer. And he was the first to distribute ski brakes, the invention that did away, finally, with leather runaway straps.

Klaus still skis Aspen every day of the season. You can't miss his flowing white mane and wide grin. "We live in our laboratory," he says, grinning, testing the feel of a new one-piece powder suit. "We're lucky. The mountains are our laboratory."

Powder poaching—
Buzzy Bent in Walsh's Gulch.
photo Robert Chamberlain

POWDER.... Skiing on clouds below your feet.

Dolores LaChapelle, erstwhile Aspen teacher and ski bum, says in her book, *Deep Powder Snow*: "One can never be bored by powder skiing because it is a special gift of the relationship between earth and sky. It only comes in sufficient amounts in particular places, at certain times on this earth; it lasts only a limited amount of time before sun or wind changes it. People devote their lives to it... To ski powder well," she says, "you must turn yourself over to the snow."

The poetry of powder snow— a state of grace between skier and earth. The skier is Fred Iselin, the powder morning many years ago. But it's the same powder poetry today …and tomorrow. photo Ferenc Berko

BY THE EARLY 1980s, powder within the ski area boundaries had, like Aspen real estate, become valuable beyond all ken. Because it was so rare. Not rare in a meteorological sense, but rare in that one seldom found an unbroken stretch of it after about 10 o'clock on a new-snow morning. Backcountry powder, on the other hand—with its infinite variations, including sugar snow, corn snow, sun crust, wind crust, peach fuzz, talcum and champagne—never got skied out.

And so, growing numbers of skiers took to the high country on telemark or touring gear looking for wild snow and an experience related to, if not exactly like, what the 10th Mountain Division troops found forty years before. Architect, dreamer and 10th Mountain veteran Fritz Benedict had never stopped skiing in the backcountry around Aspen. And now he had an idea "to help preserve a kind of simple enjoyment of the mountains." Why not build a wilderness trail in honor of the troops that would connect Aspen and Vail across the mountains? And why not build a series of huts, the way the Europeans had, each about a day's ski from the next, so that people could traverse this high country in relative comfort and safety?

The lure of the backcountry—
touring skiers beneath the Maroon Bells, in upper Maroon Creek,
the drainage that separates Aspen Highlands and Buttermilk, near Aspen.
photo David Hiser

In a remarkably short time Fritz transferred his enthusiasm to the Forest Service, to local skiers, fundraisers, volunteer builders and trail cutters. The first two cabins, designed by Benedict with bunks for about 18 skiers, with wood-burning cook stoves and solar lights and huge views into the Holy Cross Wilderness, opened for the winter of 1981-82. Now there are 16 huts—11 of them operated by the non-profit 10th Mountain Division Hut Association—in a rough, 300 mile circle linking Aspen, Vail, Leadville and the Camp Hale site at Pando. Twenty thousand people a year stay at the huts for everything from a quick overnight to two-week circumnavigations of the full loop.

Former Secretary of Defense Robert McNamara skied to Margy's Hut with Fritz on New Year's Eve, 1986. He left this entry in the hut log: "Jupiter and Mars at night…Biscuits and bourbon…plans for the future: 1) High Altitude Hyper Thermic Wellness Test Facility (sauna). 2) Solutions to economic and physical woes of Aspen/Snowmass and the rest of the world. 3) Next trip."

The next new hut will be the Fritz Benedict Hut. Fritz passed away in 1995. He was still plying the trails at 11,000 feet well into his 80th year. He loved the powder, even when it skied more like stale crusts than whipped cream. He'd come back every time and say, "God, it was great! It was just so wonderful to be out there!"

10th Mountain Trail—
skiers leave
Margy's Hut
in a gathering
storm....
photo David Hiser

85

ANOTHER KIND OF CROSS-COUNTRY SKIING was taking off on the valley floor, while Fritz was gathering support for his high-country hut system. Actually, it was nothing short of a revolution driven by three things: Lycra, skating and Pisten Bulleys. Sex, flying and grooming machines.

Tight, slinky Lycra garments gave cross-country a sex appeal it dared not dream of in the wool-and-granola '70s. Skating on nordic racing skis burst on the scene when U.S. Team maverick Bill Koch beat the Scandinavians for the overall World Cup in 1982. Kochie's prodigious use of skating made him appear, in the marvelous phrase of writer Eric Evans, to be "running on the juices of flight." And finally, for skating to be fun, you needed a wide swath of groomed track. Enter the big, fast grooming machines, borrowed at first from the downhill areas, but soon to become standard equipment at all the best nordic centers.

Nordic skating—
the new face of cross-country skiing, a graceful high-speed ballet along wide, machine packed trails.
No ski town in the West has as many nordic trails, or enthusiasts, as Aspen.
photo Team Russell

Aspen had always had track skiing, at the high school, on the golf course, out at the Snowmass Lodge and Club. It took Aspen native Craig Ward, a U.S. Team member and captain of the 1984 Olympic Team, to come home in 1982 to see the potential. Ward "got all us nordic bums together and said, 'we ought to connect all these trails,'" remembers Bob Wade, first president of the Aspen Nordic Council and one of the nordic bums. "Craig Ward had this vision and energy. He was the perfect guy to talk to these stubborn landowners (about trail easements) and to pressure the three governments: the Town of Snowmass, the City of Aspen and Pitkin County."

The city of Aspen bought two Pisten Bulleys. The county negotiated easements with developers. And before long, the various independent loops were linked: between 65 and 70 kilometers of interconnected, groomed and set track, the largest free system in the country, a self-propelled magic carpet ride some have called "Aspen's Fifth Mountain."

Aspen's Fifth Mountain—
classic cross-country, miles of track, cold air, exercise, rhythm, solitude.
The largest free public track system in the U.S.
photo John Kelly

IT'S IMPOSSIBLE to separate the story of Aspen skiing from that of racing. In 1987, Aspenite Ed McCaffrey wanted to make a statement and at the same time do something for his father, who had multiple sclerosis. He hit on the idea of an endurance race for downhillers, a test to see who could rack up the most vertical feet in a 24-hour period. That first year, at Keystone, McCaffrey and his partner Russ Klein set the standard—234,000 feet—and raised money for the National MS Society and the Jimmie Heuga Center.

From 1988 on, the race has been staged on Aspen Mountain as the Land Rover 24 Hours of Aspen, benefiting various causes from AIDS research to the Sunshine Kids. Aspen has the ultimate weapon in the Silver Queen Gondola which rises 3,267 vertical feet from the bottom of Little Nell to the top of the mountain in 13 minutes. From daylight into dark and back into day again, the two-person teams streak down Spar Gulch at nearly 80 mph, draft one another to conserve strength, try to stay focused, try to ignore their aching bodies, try above all not to fall, and then hop back in the gondola and do it all over again. And again. And again.

The 24 Hours of Aspen—
the Le Mans of ski racing, teams of two racers draft each other down Aspen Mountain, around the clock,
noon to noon, faster than we drive on a freeway. Endurance plus....
photo Burnham W. Arndt

The current record for the 24 Hours of Aspen was set in 1991 by Canadian Chris Kent (back when individual rather than team times were recognized) who went 271,161 vertical feet in 83 runs. That's over 51 vertical miles, more than 220 linear miles. The average lap from top to bottom took him two minutes and 30 seconds. The next year, 1992, as he tried to defend his title, Kent claimed that he saw a six-foot tall rabbit on the course.

Each team has a different strategy for staying alert. The 1994 hometown duo of Katie McBride and Gabriella Sutro kept their wits by taking short naps while riding up the gondola. "Right before we got to the top we would wake up and try to pep each other up," Sutro said. Other teams used hot packs on the legs, hot drinks, blankets and Eric Clapton music while they tried to get comfortable on the ride. Massage was available on certain laps.

1992 competitor Scott Nichols told a reporter just before the end, "It was like skiing by Braille; I can see a light at the end of the tunnel and, God, was it a long tunnel." Nichols' teammate Doug Coombs noted dryly, "I definitely broke my boots in." Noel Lyons, the women's record holder (along with Katie Harvey and Katie McBride) at 258,093 feet, admitted, "I had tears in my eyes on the last run. I thought that run would never come."

At the finish line: champagne and Power Bars.

Halfway through the 24 Hours of Aspen—
in the middle of the night, Katie McBride runs from her gondola car to the snow.
Teams snack and try to nap during the ride back up to the top.
photo Burnham W. Arndt

FROM THE SUNDECK RESTAURANT at the top of Aspen Mountain, the eye is inevitably drawn across Castle Creek to Highland Peak and Bowl, a monster sweep of above-timberline snow just behind the high point of Aspen Highlands ski area. The Bowl ripples with muscular, avalanche-carved shapes; it looks as if it could swallow several medium-sized ski areas. There are no tracks in the Highland Bowl powder; the alabaster shapes and blue shadows remain untouched, although the hike from the Loge Peak lift terminal appears to be a cakewalk.

In the 1970s and '80s, Highland Bowl was the number one renegade, out-of-bounds ski descent in the Aspen region. "It was because it was so visible," says Louis Dawson, one of the renegades who went on to a notable career as a mountaineer and author of guidebooks. "It had this huge mystique. We'd sneak in, leave our mark on the Bowl, go back to town and party. It was a good life, but I'm surprised I survived."

He almost didn't. One time he jumped into Main Line off the summit of Highland Peak, and a big part of the Bowl fractured around him, carrying him in an airborne avalanche hundreds of feet down the mountain. When the world stopped moving, he realized he was alive. But he'd broken both legs and would require a dangerous rescue by the Highlands ski patrol.

Avalanche control—
two patrollers prepare
to toss explosives onto
a suspect slope in the
middle of a storm.
Avalanche work is
exhausting,
painstaking and
critically important.
Problem areas like
Highland Bowl
demand years of
study before they can
be safely opened.
photo Paul Chesley

Others, less lucky, have died skiing the Bowl, and the whole area has remained very much off limits. But that may be changing. Aspen Skiing Company acquired Highlands in 1993 (now all four mountains share the same ownership), and the company has acknowledged plans to expand lift-served skiing into Highland Bowl. Not immediately, but sometime in the not-too-distant future. It is a tantalizing prospect. Lou Dawson says he would like to see it happen, even though, as he says, "as soon as it's open, it will cease to have a place in the mountaineering culture."

In fact, Aspen Highlands has not stood still—especially during the last 10 years when Highlands, and indeed all four of Aspen's ski mountains, have reinvented themselves with the help of high-speed lift technology, better grooming, new terrain and faster access to it.

New terrain, old terrain—
Aspen area skiers won't soon
run out of options, whether for
mountaineering, or on slopes
Aspen Skiing Company adds to
its white playground. Aspen
Mountain Powder Tours
already serves the bowls and
ridges behind the Sundeck;
and Highland Bowl is a
future possibility. Here we're
looking at tracks in Maroon
Bowl, the backside of
Highland Bowl, site of
guided tours in the late '60s.
photo Robert Chamberlain

Long gone is the 45 minute, shivering daydream on Aspen Mountain's No. 1 and No. 2 single chairs. Gone too is the sometimes dubious calculus at Highlands that balanced short thrills against long cat tracks and multiple-lift returns; top-to-bottom quads were Aspen Skiing Company's first present to Highlands regulars. The Tiehack flank of Buttermilk and a new Summit quad have changed the notion that Buttermilk is for beginners only; and its immaculate grooming and velvety curves have made Buttermilk a favorite Aspen hangout for "carving" snowboarders. And out west, at Snowmass, a huge mountain has grown with the times to offer one of the most modern experiences in American skiing. Highland Bowl may be the next new thing. It won't be the last.

Some dream of stitching Aspen's four mountains together with ski lifts, the way certain villages and valleys in the Alps have been interconnected. A skier could begin his day in Snowmass, say, ski to Aspen for lunch and return, over the snow, to his Snowmass digs by late afternoon. Skiing as travel: a 21st-century update of the venerable tradition.

In careful, contentious, late-20th-century Aspen, no expansion is a sure thing. But it is probably safe to say that André Roch would approve.

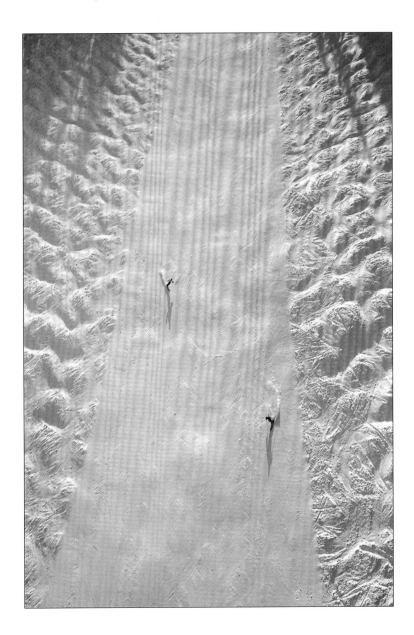

Choices, choices—
groomed snow down the
middle of Copper Bowl,
moguls to either side,
then trees and glades just
a little higher up the walls
on Gentleman's Ridge or the
backside of Bell Mountain,
and a high-speed lift
to do it all again....
photo Nicholas DeVore III

NO PEAK has a more secure place in Aspen's mountaineering pantheon than Hayden Peak, the same Hayden Peak that captivated Billy Fiske and André Roch in 1936. Halfway between Aspen and the ghostly remains of Ashcroft, 13,561 feet high, with a naked snow shoulder so perfect it works like a siren song on any skier who sees it.

Dick Jackson, a local ski and climbing guide, has walked up and skied back down Hayden at least once every year for the twenty he has been in town. Some years three or four times. He never tires of etching lines in the flawless summit snowfield, of careening down the thousand-foot Stammberger Face, banking the roller-coaster sides of the Sandy Creek drain all the way to the road, 4,000 vertical feet from the top.

"It's a showcase," he says, and he means this to be an understatement. And now in the '90s Jackson is seeing snowboarders for the first time up on Hayden. They walk up on snowshoes and then pack them away and rip down on their boards, tearing their beautiful, high-speed arcs across Hayden's pure alpine shapes.

Snowboarding—
latest reincarnation of the skiing spirit, increasingly popular on many of Aspen's slopes and peaks,
a fast learning curve, extreme angles, and the thrill of being different from your parents
(only many of Aspen's best snowboarders are in their forties and older).
photo John Kelly

"It would have been something for sure," Jackson intones, imagining the trams and trails laid out as Roch had done. But then—perhaps picturing all of the forces that influenced what Aspen did become, all of the people with their dreams and luck, the chance events and the hard work, the survivors of the "quiet years" and the energy of the newcomers—Jackson emerged from his reverie and said, "I'm just as happy as could be to have things the way they are."

He isn't alone. Aspen has come to epitomize the American success story—from rags to riches almost overnight in a setting so inspiring it drove the process with a force like inevitability. Aspen's timing was perfect. Aspen wanted to rival the great resorts of Europe, to host the biggest races and attract the most brilliant thinkers. And do it with cachet. In all of this Aspen succeeded beyond its own hopes.

There has always been competition, other towns and other ski mountains with much to recommend them. But for whole generations of skiers, wherever they grew up, Aspen—quirky, grand, obsessive and wildly successful—Aspen means skiing in America.

Plus ça change, plus c'est la même chose—

50 years later there's a beautiful continuity to the Aspen skiing experience.

Powder mornings still belong to the early birds, walking up snowy streets to the lift, today a 6-person gondola.

The town is still brick and stone and romance; the mountain still snow and sky and romance.

Everything is different. Everything is the same.

photo Burnham W. Arndt

AS ASPEN SKIING heads into its next 50 years, listen to author and long-time resident, Hunter S. Thompson:

"Aspen loves the possibility of imminent perfection and complete freedom, loves the idea that fame and fortune and beauty and truth are available to believers, and Aspen believes."

Only a memory—
but what a memory.
For generations of Aspen
skiers, Lift 1 was the start
of a healthy addiction to
snow and speed and winter,
getting to the top of a
mountain only to slide back
down to the base.
Only skiers know
how much magic is to be
found between the top of
a lift and the bottom....
photo Robert Chamberlain

CONTRIBUTORS

AUTHOR PETER SHELTON learned about Aspen skiing the right way, by doing it—lots of it.
A former ski instructor, Peter brings an insider's perspective to the craft of ski writing. He
is a contributing editor to Ski Magazine, author of *The Skier's Bible* and *The Unofficial
Guide to Skiing in the West*. Peter has thrice been voted best ski writer of the year.

PHOTOGRAPHERS
in the order in which their images appear in the book

FERENC BERKO is the dean of Aspen photographers. Born in Hungary, educated in Germany, he is
widely regarded as one of the important creative pioneers of 20th century photography.
His beautiful retrospective book, *Ferenc Berko, The Discovering Eye*, is available in Aspen
area bookstores.

BURNHAM W. ARNDT is a sculptor as well as a photographer, and often creates environmental
sculpture in the mountains and canyons around Aspen. Burnie brings a fine-art sensibility
to everything that he shoots, from landscapes to ski action.

ROBERT CHAMBERLAIN came to Aspen as a teenager in 1951. His twin passions have always been
skiing and documentary black-and-white photography. His photos are frequently featured in Aspen magazine, and he has contributed to numerous books.

MARGARET DURRANCE and her husband DICK DURRANCE are certainly "the first couple" of ski
photography in Aspen. Not merely spectators and recorders of the emerging American ski
scene, they were active participants. Dick Durrance represented the U.S. at the 1936
Winter Olympics, but that's just a small part of the Durrance saga, a story told with wit
and charm and lots of great photos in their book, *The Man on the Medal*—a must for any
serious skier's library (available at all Aspen bookstores).

DAVID HISER is a founding member of Photographers Aspen and has photographed sixty assignments for National Geographic. He sold his first photograph to Aspen Skiing Company in 1965.

MARY ESHBAUGH HAYES is a writer as well as a photographer. She has chronicled the Aspen scene in her weekly column for the Aspen Times for 40 years. Mary also publishes books and photo notecards from her West-End home.

JOHN RUSSELL has made a name for himself in sports photography with numerous national magazine cover images. He shoots tennis and stock images from Europe to Hawaii.

JUDY HILL is the guiding spirit of the Hill Gallery and lab in Aspen. She specializes in dramatic color scenics of the Aspen area and the Rocky Mountains.

TONY DEMIN, action photographer and former Aspenite, is represented by Photographers Aspen.

BOB KRUEGER calls Woody Creek home. He's a free-lance and magazine photographer who's never lost his love of black and white. His book, *Gypsy on 18 Wheels*, chronicles the life of the American trucker.

ALAN BECKER is a globe-trotting editorial and stock photographer based in Aspen. His work is represented by different agencies including Photographers Aspen.

JOHN KELLY is a remarkable "photo athlete" who specializes in capturing other athletes in strange light and strong moments. John is famous for quick reflexes and decisive composition; he's one of the most artistic sports/action photographers working today.

PAUL CHESLEY is another founding partner of Photographers Aspen, and a regular contributor to National Geographic magazine and books.

NICHOLAS DEVORE III is the third founding partner of Photographers Aspen. Like his colleagues, he has shot numerous stories for National Geographic around the globe.

ACKNOWLEDGEMENTS

Special thanks to Sara Oats at the Aspen Historical Society; Killeen Russell, Nancy Scheinkman, Bobbie Burkley and Bob Maynard of the Aspen Skiing Company; Gaylord Guenin for permission to quote from *Aspen: The Quiet Years*; Elizabeth Boyles; Dick Jackson of Aspen Expeditions; Louis W. Dawson; Bob Wade of the Aspen Nordic Council; Andy Mill; Jon Reveal; Peter Looram of the 10th Mountain Division Hut Association; Ned Ryerson; Dolores LaChapelle; and most especially to Bob "We Don't Rent Rooms to Skiers" Chamberlain.

SOURCES

Aspen: The Quiet Years, by Kathleen Krieger Daily and Gaylord T. Guenin, Red Ink Inc., 1994.

Deep Powder Snow, 40 Years of Ecstatic Skiing, Avalanches and Earth Wisdom, by Dolores LaChapelle, Kivakí Press, 1993.

Famous Aspen, by Caroline Bancroft, Johnson Publishing Company, 1951.

The Man on the Medal: The Life & Times of America's First Great Ski Racer, by Dick Durrance as told to John Jerome, Durrance Enterprises, Inc., 1995.

Nice Goin': My Life On Skis, by Friedl Pfeifer with Morten Lund, Pictorial Histories Publishing Company, Inc., 1993.

Re-Creation Through Recreation: Aspen Skiing From 1870 to 1970, by Anne Gilbert, Aspen Historical Society, 1995.

The Romance of Commerce and Culture: Capitalism, Modernism, and the Chicago-Aspen Crusade for Cultural Reform, by James Sloan Allen, The University of Chicago Press, 1983.

Skiing Pioneers, by Rick Richards, Dry Gulch Publishing, 1992

ASPEN SKIING

THE FIRST FIFTY YEARS

is published by
Western Eye Press
Box 917, Telluride CO 81435
in conjunction with the
Aspen Skiing Company

Text ©1996 Peter Shelton.
Copyright for all the photographs
is retained by the individual photographers.
Title-page photograph: aspen trunk and
shadows by Burnham W. Arndt.

ISBN 0-941283-14-3 hardbound

Designed and edited by Lito Tejada-Flores.
Printed in Hong Kong
by Pacific Rim International.
Production coordination, Tommy Lee.

Readers wishing to purchase prints of some of
the beautiful historic photographs reproduced
in this book may be interested in contacting
the Aspen Historical Society which has
produced a handsome catalog of available
historic photos.